EVEN AS MY SOUL PROSPERS
NOT SO SUBTLE REMINDERS THAT GOD WANTS YOU TO PROSPER

ALLISON DENISE ARNETT

BRAND IT BEAUTIFULLY™ * HOUSTON, TX

Copyright © 2022 by Allison Denise Arnett

All rights reserved.

No part of this book may be reproduced, stored, or transmitted by any means - whether auditory, graphic, mechanical, or electronic - without written permission of both publisher and author, except in the case of brief excerpts used in critical articles and certain other noncommercial uses permitted by copyright law. Unauthorized reproduction of any part of this work is illegal and is punishable by law.

Unless otherwise notated, scripture quotations are taken from the Holy Bible, New Living Translation, copyright ©1996, 2004, 2015 by Tyndale House Foundation. Used by permission of Tyndale House Publishers, Carol Stream, Illinois 60188. All rights reserved. Printed and bound in the United States of America

Paperback ISBN: 978-1-7354763-5-3

Book Designed and Published by Brand It Beautifully™

www.branditbeautifully.com

allison@imallisondenise.com

To every Christian leader holding firm to their faith.

Beloved, I pray that in every way you may succeed and prosper and be in good health [physically], just as [I know] your soul prospers [spiritually]. 3 John 1:2

CONTENTS

Acknowledgments	vii
Foreword Patti Denise Henry	ix
Introduction Allison Denise Arnett	xi
Financial Prosperity	1
Spiritual Prosperity	33
Physical Prosperity	69
Encourage One Another	103
More Encouragement	129

ACKNOWLEDGMENTS

I am grateful to each contributing author with whom I have had the pleasure of collaborating with for this sacred work. Thank You, Holy Spirit, for the divine inspiration and guidance. Thank you to my family for your patience and understanding as I labored to prepare this written work. What we are doing will last generations.

FOREWORD
PATTI DENISE HENRY

 What shall it profit a man if he shall gain the whole world and lose his own soul? - Mark 8:36

In my line of work, I have come across many spiritually hungry souls seeking healing in their bodies and abundance in their bank accounts. They fail to see that what they have truly failed to feed is their souls. The key phrase in the founding scripture of this book, 3 John 1:2, is "even as your soul prospers." Even as means, in the same way, while, or just as. Which means your financial, wellness, and spiritual prosperity should be growing in congruence with each other. A two-legged stool can not stand as strongly as a three-legged stool, and a "threefold cord is not easily broken." True prosperity is equal to a soul whose *whole* being is prospering. Soul work is God's work and God wants to work on your being because it profits you nothing to gain the whole world and lose your own soul. I partner with God and with the authors of this transformational book to share tools to encourage you and remind you that even when we face a dark night of the soul, God still wants us to prosper in every way.

ABOUT PATTI DENISE HENRY:

A native of the Island of Trinidad & Tobago, Patti is internationally recognized as a Minister, Psalmist, Teacher, Hospice Chaplain, Family & Bereavement Counselor, Published Author and Prolific Speaker. She is also known as "A Prophetic Worshiper" as her sound in the earth impacts the heart and mind of all who come into contact with her ministry.

Patti Henry uses Biblical insight along with life experiences to help you to identify "The Holes in Your Soul" and provide the necessary tools to transform you into "Beautiful Souls".

She is the Founder & President of He Restores My Soul, LLC and Sisters, Let's Keep Talking! Patti is humbled by the call that God has placed on her life and is very passionate about her purpose which is to multiply disciples for Christ and to function as a soul coach where she motivates others to live before they die. She is indeed a servant leader for such a time as this.

INTRODUCTION
ALLISON DENISE ARNETT

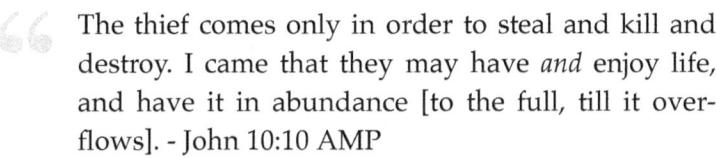
> The thief comes only in order to steal and kill and destroy. I came that they may have *and* enjoy life, and have it in abundance [to the full, till it overflows]. - John 10:10 AMP

In today's climate, it can feel like we can't win for losing. It can feel like the thief is doing everything to steal and kill and destroy our hope and our joy. Talks of recession, sickness, and pain can leave us feeling anxious and barren.

But our Word tells us that we need not be concerned with the cares of this world because our God has overcome this world. He came that we would have life and have it more abundantly!

Even as My Soul Prospers is a beacon call, a reminder, that God wants us to succeed and to prosper in EVERY way — even when it seems the world is hardening around us. This book is meant to be a tool for the Holy Spirit to breathe life back into the places where you feel less than abundant. Read it through thoughtfully. Then read it again… every time you need a not so subtle reminder that God *still* wants you to succeed in every way.

FINANCIAL PROSPERITY

I PRAY THAT IN EVERY WAY YOU MAY SUCCEED AND PROSPER.

PROSPER:

1 to grant a prosperous and expeditious journey, to lead by a direct and easy way

2 to grant a successful issue, to cause to prosper

3 to prosper, be successful

succeed in reaching; figuratively, to succeed in business affairs:— (have a) prosper

— Lexicon :: Strong's G2137 - euodoō

I CHOOSE TO GIVE GENEROUSLY SO THAT I MAY REAP ABUNDANTLY

A PROSPERITY MOMENT
WITH CIARA SHANAE

> The generous soul will be made rich, And he who waters will also be watered himself. ~ Proverbs 11:25 NKJV

I REMEMBER HEARING conversations where believers were questioning why some non-believers appeared to be so blessed with riches. The thing is — God's word is true and impartial. It works no matter who's working it. A biblical principle that I have seen work in my life is, "give and you shall receive." During seasons where I needed the most, God urged me to help, serve, and give more. It did not make sense to me but I listened and as a result, I received a miraculous monetary gift.

There are many "get rich quick" schemes but, the quickest way to get rich is through generosity. Thank God He is generous with His breath of life, His riches in glory, and His love. Do not get weary in well-doing (Galatians 6:9). Instead pray, give, network, trust, and watch God work!

AFFIRMATION: I CHOOSE TO GIVE GENEROUSLY SO THAT I MAY REAP ABUNDANTLY.

LIFE IS TOUGH
BUT I AM
TOUGHER
BECAUSE GOD
CREATED ME !

A PROSPERITY MOMENT
WITH CLARICE MAY CREGGER

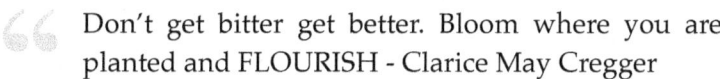 Don't get bitter get better. Bloom where you are planted and FLOURISH - Clarice May Cregger

IN ISAIAH 35:1-2 God said, "the wilderness and the dry land shall be glad; the desert shall rejoice and blossom like the crocus; it shall blossom abundantly and rejoice with joy and singing." Life is tough, yes, but you are tougher. God created you for a purpose so do not quit because it is getting harder. If anything, push harder because God planted those visions, dreams, and goals in your heart for a reason. When challenges and opposition arise be excited and embrace them because it is an indicator that you are on the right path. The path to success is narrow but do not grow weary. You may not see the outcome yet, but God is already orchestrating everything for you. All you have to do is be you, show up, do your best, and leave the rest to God.

AFFIRMATION: LIFE IS TOUGH BUT I AM TOUGHER BECAUSE GOD CREATED ME!

PROSPERITY AND WEALTH ARE MINE TO INHERIT

A PROSPERITY MOMENT
WITH CLARISSA PRITCHETT

> But remember the LORD your God, for it is he who gives you the ability to produce wealth, and so confirms his covenant, which he swore to your ancestors, as it is today. - Deuteronomy 8:18 (NIV)

YOU ARE a leader that walks towards prosperity and wealth. Open yourself up to the fact that abundance is everywhere as our Almighty God is omnipresent. Prosperity and wealth is for everyone to inherit, produce, and enjoy. View yourself as prosperous and wealthy. When you wake each morning count your blessings and plan to prosper. Gratitude will guide you in your goals. Plant seeds of prosperity in your heart and mind and water those seeds with God's word when your life feels dry. Focus on taking action that will benefit you today and tomorrow. Stay away from distractions that slow you down. Focus your attention on what your heart truly desires and what God swore to your ancestors. Notice prosperity and wealth around you and remember that success is within your reach!

AFFIRMATION: PROSPERITY AND WEALTH ARE MINE TO INHERIT.

MY FORTUNE BEGINS WITH MY THINKING!

A PROSPERITY MOMENT
WITH REV. CURTIS THATCHER

 Reframe your thinking. - Rev. Curtis Thatcher

IT IS a defining moment in your life when you realize the great truth that while things happen around you and to you, the only things that truly matter are the things that happen within you. You have little control over the environment, stock market fluctuations, or other people's conduct. However, you live in a world of your awareness, which is the sum total of your mind's thoughts. And you have influence over what happens in your head. This is not to imply it is simple, but to demonstrate that it is achievable.

The Bible states that many of Jesus' disciples withdrew and stopped following him when He started to outline the strict rules of His teaching *(John 6:66 KJV)* and it's still true today. However, if you are prepared to take full responsibility for your actions, you may alter your life's experiences through a change in awareness, just as your level of thinking has contributed to where you are now.

AFFIRMATION: MY FORTUNE BEGINS WITH MY THINKING!

GOD KEEPS ME AND PROVIDES FOR ME.

A PROSPERITY MOMENT
WITH DEBORAH RIVERS DECOTEAU

> Trust in the Lord with all your heart. Lean not on your own understanding. In all your ways acknowledge him and he will direct your path. - Proverbs 3:5-6

LIFE MAY NOT ALWAYS GO the way we want it to, but know that God will always be with you. I remember being a single mom of five, working Monday through Friday and some Saturdays and found myself drowning in financial difficulties. There were days I did not know if I would be able to feed my household or pay my rent and utilities. Most nights I fell asleep in tears — until I learned to give my burdens to the Lord in prayer.

I can look back over my life and say with personal conviction that God has never disappointed me and I have gained the utmost respect for my Provider. My children and I were never homeless, hungry or naked. Trust Him to keep and provide for you, too. He will do it.

AFFIRMATION: GOD KEEPS ME AND PROVIDES FOR ME.

WHEN I GIVE, MY BLESSINGS ARE MULTIPLIED!

A PROSPERITY MOMENT
WITH GEMMA BROWNE

> Give, and it will be given to you; a good measure—pressed down, shaken together, and running over—will be poured into your lap. For with the measure you use, it will be measured back to you. - Luke 6:38 HCSB

WE AS BELIEVERS of the body of Christ sometimes struggle with our finances. Luke 6:38 says "give and it will be given to you." This means we have a part to play. Take every opportunity to give and do good because you may be the answer to someone's prayer. When we serve God by serving others, God multiplies it back to us. So don't hold back because you fear you may run out of resources. Joshua 1:8 says '"we should always mediate on the scriptures, then do what it says, for that is the way to be prosperous and successful." Well the Word clearly says to "give." So when we give as we've been instructed, we position ourselves to receive blessings from God. Get in position — a giver's position.

AFFIRMATION: WHEN I GIVE, MY BLESSINGS ARE MULTIPLIED!

I ALIGN WITH
THE FLOW OF
THE
SOLUTION.

A PROSPERITY MOMENT
WITH JANENE DHALAI

> And if it seem evil unto you to serve the Lord, choose you this day whom ye will serve; - Joshua 24:15a KJV

FINANCIAL CRISES, even recessions or depressions, begin with your reactions of faith or fear, insofar as they touch your wallet, bank account, or job stability. Although we all share in the collective consciousness that causes economic conditions, you are not the cause. If, however, you give them reality by having negative thoughts or conversations about them, you become synchronized with an energy flow that has the same immediate impact on your life as the light that comes on when you flip the switch. You do not create the light, but it becomes real in your experience as a result of your act of turning it on. As such, your prosperity begins with you. What happens in your thinking and is mirrored in your affairs will have an impact on the world's affairs. You are either on the side of the issue or on the side of the solution. Choose the side of the solution.

AFFIRMATION: I ALIGN WITH THE FLOW OF THE SOLUTION.

MY FINANCES ARE BLESSED BECAUSE I'M A HEARER AND A DOER OF THE WORD.

A PROSPERITY MOMENT
WITH LINDA KENNARD

> This book of the law shall not depart out of thou mouth but thou shall meditate therein day and night that thou mayest observe to do according to all that is written therein for then thou shall make thy way prosperous and then thou shalt have good success. - Joshua 1:8

YOUR FINANCES BEGIN to grow as you sow. Meditate on God's Word and decree it! You will have what you say. His Word never returns void; it always prospers. God strategically places people around you so you and they can be blessed. Trust the process and don't lean to what you think or understand.

God was the first investor when He sowed His only begotten Son. Jesus was the first network marketer by choosing the disciples to repeat His process and make disciples. When He gave talents to men, the two who stepped out in faith and invested for a return doubled their blessing and were rewarded.

AFFIRMATION: MY FINANCES ARE BLESSED BECAUSE I'M A HEARER AND A DOER OF THE WORD.

I FORGIVE ME BECAUSE CHRIST HAS MADE ME DEBT FREE !

A PROSPERITY MOMENT
WITH MONIQUE MOORER

SO MANY THINGS have happened in our past. Many great and wonderful memories that may be marred by decisions we've made that we are not proud of. The enemy wants us to feel shackled and restrained by the things we keep hidden in our secret place and are ashamed to share. He desires to "steal, kill and destroy" our spirits. Let's no longer allow the enemy to keep us in the bondage of our history.

We are not what we have been through, but survivors of it. Our past does not define us. We must forgive ourselves of our choices and our decisions. Let's use what we have encountered as an avenue to inspire others to realize that their latter shall be greater. 1 John 1:9 AMPC reminds us that "if we [freely] admit that we have sinned and confess our sins, He is faithful and just (true to His own nature and promises) and will forgive our sin." Repenting to God and knowing that we are free is liberating. If our all-knowing and all-seeing God can forgive us because of Christ's ultimate sacrifice, let us now begin to forgive ourselves.

AFFIRMATION: I FORGIVE ME BECAUSE CHRIST HAS MADE ME DEBT FREE!

I PRAY BIG AND GOD DELIVERS EVEN BIGGER.

A PROSPERITY MOMENT
WITH NADIA MORALES

> What no eye has seen, what no ear has heard, and what no human mind has conceived the things God has prepared for those who love him. - 1 Corinthians 2:9 NIV

WHEN I WAS in my 20s, a family situation changed the trajectory of my life. I had to support my family – all 4 of us – while I was just starting my career as a newly licensed chemist. I was praying for the ability to earn enough for shelter, utilities, part of my brother's college tuition, and food. I prayed for the bare necessities. Have you ever done that — prayed small prayers? I prayed small because I was unknowingly relying on myself. God revealed to me that He chose us to do hard things, so we would acknowledge that it's not us who made it possible, but Him and Him alone. Let's lay claim to His promises and pray for bigger, greater things, expecting Him to go above and beyond for us because we love Him.

AFFIRMATION: I PRAY BIG AND GOD DELIVERS EVEN BIGGER.

GOD GIVES ME THE POWER TO GET WEALTH AND I WILL HONOR HIM!

A PROSPERITY MOMENT
WITH MINISTER PESHON ALLEN

> Everything we have and that we think we've gained ourselves comes from God. - Mr. Tyron A. Allen

SUCCESS COMES IN MANY FORMS. Some people look at success as having a lot of money and material things. Others look at it as having great peace and being content in life. But here's the thing, God wants us to have good success in *all things* in life. The key is not to make that success an idol. The Bible speaks about money and teaches us to be a good steward over it. With everything we have we should be like King Solomon and ask God for wisdom so we can steward our finances God's way. Turn your finances, your career, and family over to God and trust Him to guide you and give you good success in your finances. Follow the Lord's strategy and His plans and walk where He leads you. You will have to do the work, but God will give you the plans and the way. Trust and follow his leading.

AFFIRMATION: GOD GIVES ME THE POWER TO GET WEALTH AND I WILL HONOR HIM!

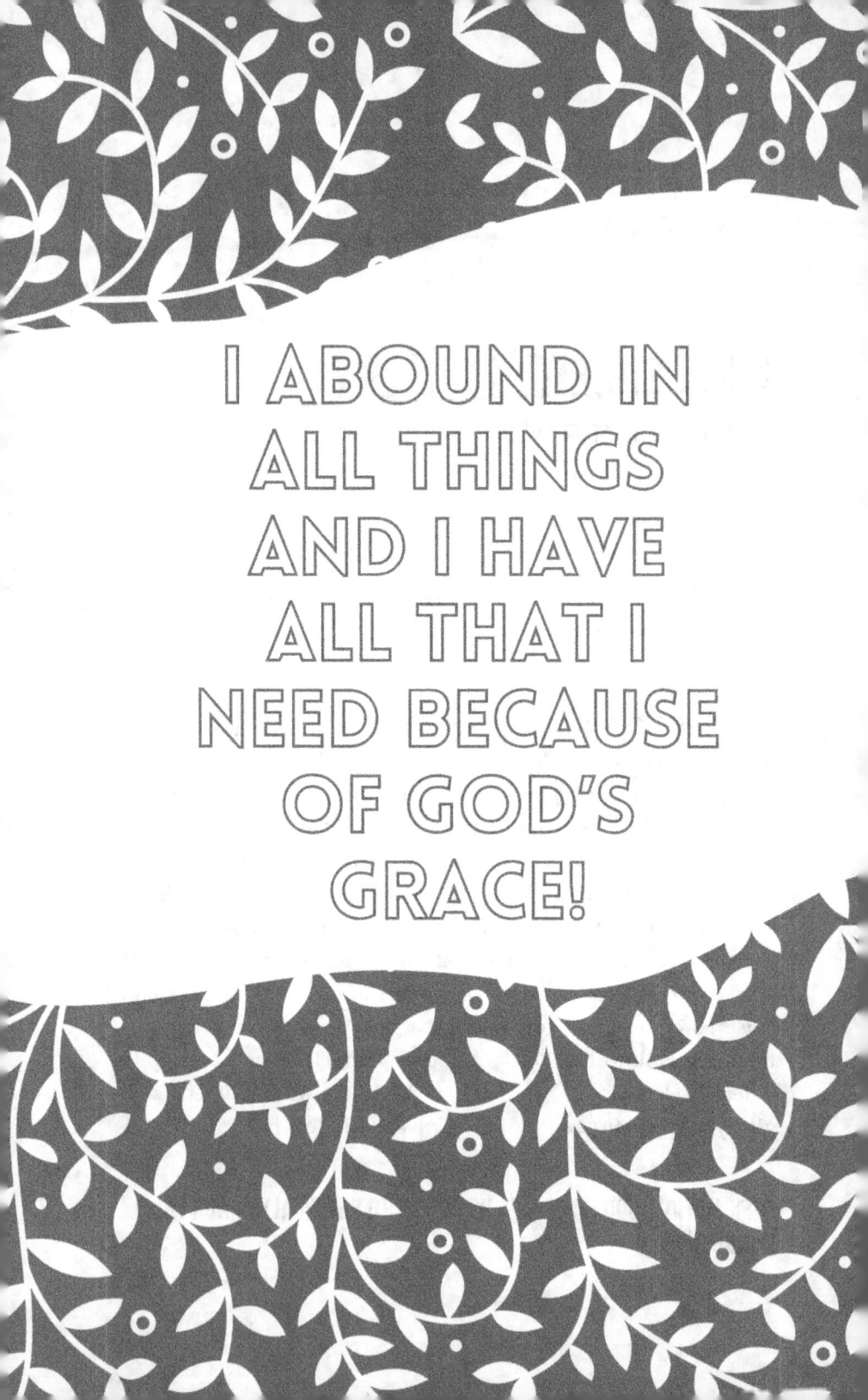

A PROSPERITY MOMENT
WITH SHANDRA PARKS

> And God is able to bless you abundantly, so that in all things at all times, having all that you need, you will abound in every good work." (2 Corinthians 9:8)

ABOUNDING IN ALL THINGS! Each season brings us lessons. Each season comes with peaks and valleys. But in spite of what it looks or feels like, we are abounding in all things. We are thriving. We are more than conquerors. We are complete. We are victorious. We must remember that we are surrounded by grace (unmerited favor). This grace plays a big part in us prospering financially. So change your perspective about your life. Affirm the promises of God over your life and finances. Declare God's grace over your life and finances. Settle for nothing less than abounding in all things.

AFFIRMATION: I ABOUND IN ALL THINGS AND I HAVE ALL THAT I NEED BECAUSE OF GOD'S GRACE!

A PROSPERITY MOMENT
WITH DR. TSCHANNA TAYLOR

> But first *and* most importantly seek (aim at, strive after) His kingdom and His righteousness [His way of doing and being right—the attitude and character of God], and all these things will be given to you also. - Matthew 6:33 AMP

GOD WANTS us to prosper in every way — body, spirit, health, mind, and finances. Philippians 4:19 tells us that "God shall supply all our needs according to His riches in glory by Christ Jesus," however we are to be faithful stewards with our finances.

Do you put your faith in your bank account or your paycheck? Neither of these are your source. Do you fear that He will fail you? Belief in God means you trust Him. Trusting Him opens your trust account in heaven and opens many blessings over your life from which you can withdraw from like a checking account. God will provide. Every time. Do you trust Him?

AFFIRMATION: BECAUSE I TRUST GOD, I CAN LIVE TODAY AND NOT WORRY ABOUT TOMORROW.

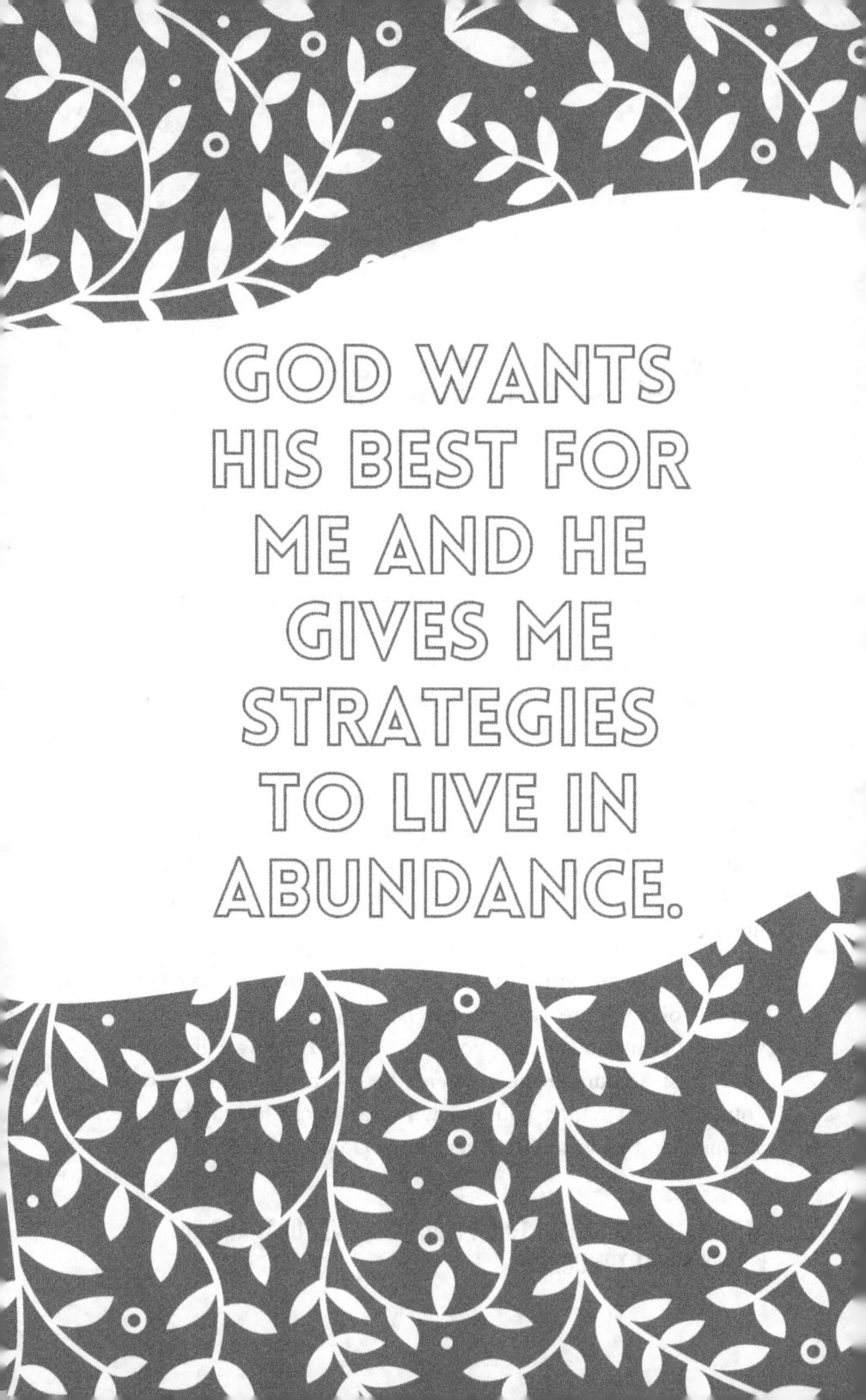

A PROSPERITY MOMENT
WITH TYRIA D. JONES

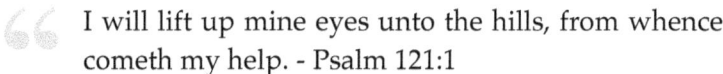
I will lift up mine eyes unto the hills, from whence cometh my help. - Psalm 121:1

SOMETIMES WHAT WE see with our physical eyes doesn't line up with what we know God has promised. We don't understand why we're struggling when we're doing all that we can do to make things work. Instead of looking at your own means, I encourage you to look to Him because He has everything that you need. We are reminded of this in Ephesians 3:20, "Now unto him that is able to do exceeding abundantly above all that we ask or think, according to the power that worketh in us."

It is not God's will for us to live paycheck to paycheck or for us to be in a financial situation where we are "robbing Peter to pay Paul". He desires that we live in prosperity because everything we need is found in Him. Surrender it all to Him and allow Him to give you a strategy for your finances.

AFFIRMATION: GOD WANTS HIS BEST FOR ME AND HE GIVES ME STRATEGIES TO LIVE IN ABUNDANCE.

SPIRITUAL PROSPERITY
I PRAY THAT YOUR SOUL PROSPERS

SOUL:

1 the seat of the feelings, desires, affections, aversions (our heart, soul etc.)

2 the (human) soul in so far as it is constituted that by the right use of the aids offered it by God it can attain its highest end and secure eternal blessedness, the soul regarded as a moral being designed for everlasting life

3 the soul as an essence which differs from the body and is not dissolved by death (distinguished from other parts of the body)

— Lexicon :: Strong's G5590 - psychē

I HAVE THE FAITH TO FINISH IT!

A PROSPERITY MOMENT
WITH CEDRIC STANTON

> Faith is building on what you know is here, so you can reach what you know is there. - Cullen Hightower

MANY TIMES, we start on a plan with excitement, high expectations, and connections because they present great results. It is normal to feel like quitting when working with a plan that has a future—but a plan without faith is dead. Millions of times when we have these feelings, it is base on dreams and ideas that we put together. It sounds inspiring, but when that metaphorical rock cracks the windshield of life, it shatters our expectation to pieces leaving us feeling like we do not have the faith to finish. James 2:26 NIV says, "As the body without the spirit is dead, so faith without deeds is dead." Hebrews 11:6 NIV says, "And without faith it is impossible to please God, because anyone who comes to him must believe that he exists and that he rewards those who earnestly seek him." Start believing God's best for what you're building so you can finish it.

AFFIRMATION: I HAVE THE FAITH TO FINISH IT!

GOD IS MY BEST FRIEND AND I ENJOY SPENDING TIME WITH HIM.

A PROSPERITY MOMENT
WITH CIARA SHANAE

> *This Book of the Law shall not depart from your mouth, but you shall meditate in it day and night, that you may observe to do according to all that is written in it. For then you will make your way prosperous, and then you will have good success.* ~Joshua 1:8 NKJV

I ALWAYS THOUGHT of this verse very literally for Joshua. But what if we looked at it in a more modern way, such as, having daily conversations with God? Spending time in God's Word definitely gives my spirit life and weakens my flesh so I'm still an advocate for mediating on His Word. However, even if you may not read the Word each and every day, you can still have daily conversations with God. Speak to Him then be still and anticipate His response. Putting actions to the strategies He gives you in His responses will prosper every aspect of your life! Commune with God and allow Him to show you the way to your land of milk and honey.

AFFIRMATION: GOD IS MY BEST FRIEND AND I ENJOY SPENDING TIME WITH HIM.

I LET GO AND TRUST GOD'S PROCESS.

A PROSPERITY MOMENT
WITH CLARICE MAY CREGGER

 Trust in the Lord with all your heart and lean not on your own understanding; - Proverbs 3:5

TAKE a deep breath and take life one day at a time. Life can be overwhelming and mentally taxing, but the good news is we are not doing life alone. God is always with us and he would never give us more than what we can handle. He will never leave you, nor forsake you. God said, "Fear not, for I am with you; be not dismayed, for I am your God; I will strengthen you, I will help you, I will uphold you with my righteous right hand." Deuteronomy 31:8. All you must do when in doubt is be still and trust the process.

AFFIRMATION: I LET GO AND TRUST GOD'S PROCESS.

GOD IS
PLEASED
WHEN ALL IS
GOING WELL
FOR ME.

A PROSPERITY MOMENT
WITH CLARISSA PRITCHETT

> I pray that you may prosper in all things and be in health, just as your soul prospers. – John 1:2 (NKJV)

GOD'S RESOURCES ARE LIMITLESS. Prosperity is more than finances. May your heart, mind, and spirit be at peace daily knowing that your life has purpose. Find comfort and strength in the spiritual gifts God wants you to use to prosper in your purpose. God wants to bless your life and He delights in your prosperity. The bible says, "Let them call out for joy and be glad, who want to see the thing done for me. Let them always say, "May the Lord be honored. He is pleased when all is going well for His servant." (Psalm 35:27). Accept Jesus as your Savior and make Him the center of your life. Call out for His joy and be glad in your soul! Then you will prosper in all things and be in good health, even as your soul prospers!

AFFIRMATION: GOD IS PLEASED WHEN ALL IS GOING WELL FOR ME.

A PROSPERITY MOMENT
WITH REV. CURTIS THATCHER

> The Lord has directed your steps. - Rev. Curtis Thatcher

ALLOW nature to remind you that everything has a season. Bright red or yellow apples began as a compact bud of promise, blossomed into a lovely springtime flower, then ripened into a tasty and healthy fruit ready for harvest. Each stage of the apple's development was ordered and necessary for completion. Order is active in your life as well. Be inspired by ideas that follow an ordered road to realization. Allow your thoughts to mature, foster them with thinking and consideration, and then act constructively. Seek God's guidance and try to work in accordance with the divine order of the creative process. There is a season for everything, and a time for everything under heaven— (Ecclesiastes 3:1 KJV)

AFFIRMATION: AS I GAIN SPIRITUAL INSIGHT, I FLOW WITH GOD'S DIVINE CREATIVE PROCESS.

I AM SPIRIT-FILLED AND PRODUCING GOOD FRUIT.

A PROSPERITY MOMENT
WITH DEBORAH RIVERS DECOTEAU

 Wherefore by their fruits ye shall know them. - Matt. 7:15-20

WHAT DOES it mean to be spiritual or to live a Spirit-filled life? Going to church, giving to the poor, reading the bible and memorizing bible verses?

Believing that Jesus Christ is the son of God and building a genuine relationship with Him is the beginning of living a Spirit-filled life. Genuine belief in Jesus Christ as your Savior will cause you to be filled with the Holy Spirit. The Holy Spirit will then counsel, comfort, guide, chastise, and make intercession for you unto GOD.

Because "a good tree cannot bring forth evil fruit; neither can a corrupt tree bring forth good fruit," you will know you are living a Spirit-filled life when the following show up in your interactions with people: "love, joy, peace, patience, kindness, goodness, faithfulness, gentleness, and self-control."

AFFIRMATION: I AM SPIRIT-FILLED AND PRODUCING GOOD FRUIT.

GOD HAS MY BACK SO I CHOOSE PEACE !

A PROSPERITY MOMENT
WITH GEMMA BROWNE

> I don't say this out of need, for I have learned to be content in whatever circumstances I am. - Philippians 4:11

TRIALS AND TROUBLES may arise but God gives us the ability to overcome them. He calls us "more than conquerors" after all! When we surrender and put our complete trust in God, our life turns in a whole new direction. Make an effort to have your mind and body in a continuous state of praise. Continuously offer up gratitude and thanksgiving to tap into that place of peace within your soul. Rest in Him knowing that He cares for you and is causing all things to work together for your good (Romans 8:28). Draw near to Him and He will draw near to you. What am I really saying here? I am saying that God has your back so you don't have to live in stress or worry. Choose gratitude! Choose contentment. Choose peace!

AFFIRMATION: GOD HAS MY BACK SO I CHOOSE PEACE!

BECAUSE OF MY SPIRITUAL UNDERSTANDING, I KNOW MORE THAN WHAT THE EYE CAN SEE.

A PROSPERITY MOMENT
WITH JANENE DHALAI

> Give therefore thy servant an understanding heart to judge thy people, that I may discern between good and bad: for who is able to judge this thy so. - 1 Kings 3:9KJV

SPIRITUALIZED UNDERSTANDING IS a precious jewel that taps into the bottomless well of compassion. It gently takes us below the facts of life—the situations, feelings, and ways we see things—to a better way of seeing.

Spiritual understanding comes from looking for it and realizing that human understanding alone does not always lead to good results. In order to make sweet lemonade out of lemons, we use our spiritual knowledge. In his time, the Bible's King Solomon was thought to be one of the wisest and wealthiest people. He only asked God for one thing. He asked for a heart of understanding so that he could judge God's people and so he could tell the difference between good and evil.(1 Kings 3:9KJV).

AFFIRMATION: BECAUSE OF MY SPIRITUAL UNDERSTANDING, I KNOW MORE THAN WHAT THE EYE CAN SEE.

I WILL LOVE THE LORD WITH ALL MY HEART, SOUL, STRENGTH, AND MIND.

A PROSPERITY MOMENT
WITH LINDA KENNARD

> " He that dwelleth in the secret place of the Most High God, shall abide under the shadow of the Almighty. - Psalms 91:1

WHEN YOU ARE DWELLING in that secret place, it can not be compared to any other place. Abiding under the shadow of His presence changes your entire being: spirit, soul, and body.

To be successful in your spiritual walk with God, it takes having an intimate relationship with Him. Get to know Him through daily conversation with Him (prayer) and His word. Offer Him your flesh, the body, Rom 12:1 (the outer courts), then the soul (will, mind, and emotions which is the Holy Place), and the spiritual realm (Holy of Holies). Beautiful things happen there such as: intimacy, birthing, breakthroughs, submission, losing fleshly desires, deep conversations, revelations, and so much more. Praise and worship can also be used as spiritual weapons as God inhabits the praises of His people (Psalm 22:3).

AFFIRMATION: I WILL LOVE THE LORD WITH ALL MY HEART, SOUL, STRENGTH, AND MIND.

ANXIOUSNESS
NO LONGER
LIVES HERE.
I EMBRACE
PEACE.

A PROSPERITY MOMENT
WITH MONIQUE MOORER

FEAR COMMONLY SHOWS up as anxiousness — the sense of always looking over your shoulder or worrying about different circumstances. Its main origin is usually traumatic or high stress situations. We feel a lack of control. There may be a feeling of restlessness which can cause a feeling of panic leaving you frozen in fear. It's like being in a scary movie and when something jumps out at you, instead of running, you stand in one spot screaming and crying; unable to move. But your movie doesn't have to end right there.

When we are in Christ Jesus, there is a sweet calmness in knowing that God has given us every tool we need to deal with everything we may encounter. In 2 Timothy 1:7 NLT we are reminded that "God has not given us a spirit of fear, but of power, love and of a sound mind." God wants our spirit, mind, body, and soul to be at peace. He wants us to remember that this peace is found in spending time in His Word where we can find everything we need to put our fears to rest.

AFFIRMATION: ANXIOUSNESS NO LONGER LIVES HERE. I EMBRACE PEACE.

GOD IS FIGHTING FOR ME AND I AM NEVER ALONE.

A PROSPERITY MOMENT
WITH NADIA MORALES

> He will call on me, and I will answer him; I will be with him in trouble, I will deliver him and honor him. – Psalm 91:15

WHEN WE SAY yes to God, we leave everything behind. This is why we struggle as humans – not because His yoke isn't easy and His burden isn't light, but because we deliberately choose to pick up our cross and go for what He has called us to do. Sometimes, it's as easy as donating your old clothes to a homeless shelter, but oftentimes, it's as hard as saying no to what the world has to offer to be bold in who we are in Christ.

This struggle is like light rain that turns into a storm, destroying our ship and leaving us swimming in cold, dark waters. It gets bigger – bigger than us, bigger than what we had expected, bigger than what we normally can handle. The good thing is our God walks on water. As you call His name, He answers. With His grace, you'll pull through. He's always with you.

AFFIRMATION: GOD IS FIGHTING FOR ME AND I AM NEVER ALONE.

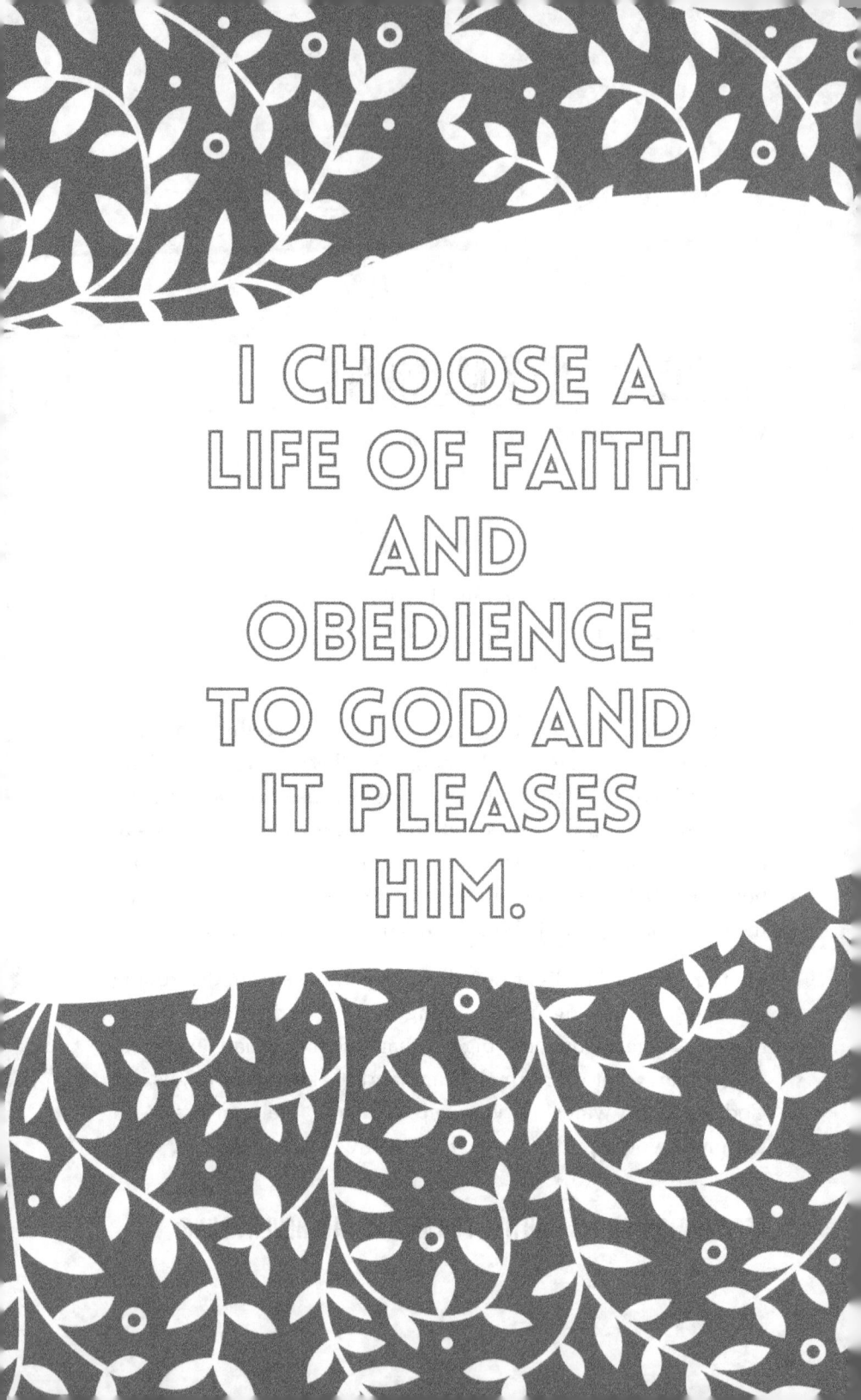

A PROSPERITY MOMENT
WITH MINISTER PESHON ALLEN

> " Your lying dormant hinders your success and gives your enemy an opportunity to rejoice." - Dr. Vinita Johnson

IT MAY BE hard to imagine that God, wants an intimate relationship with us, but He does. It's the reason He created us. Everyday God is with us and for us and has a cloud of witnesses cheering us on to the finish line. Be encouraged. God loves all of us more than we will ever really know. Draw closer to Him by reading His Word, praying to Him, listening to what He says to your heart, and expressing your faith through obedience.

Hebrews 11:5-6 states, "By faith Enoch was translated that he should not see death; and was not found, because God had translated him: for before his translation he had this testimony, that he pleased God. But without faith it is impossible to please him: for he that cometh to God must believe that he is, and that he is a rewarder of them that diligently seek him."

AFFIRMATION: I CHOOSE A LIFE OF FAITH AND OBEDIENCE TO GOD AND IT PLEASES HIM.

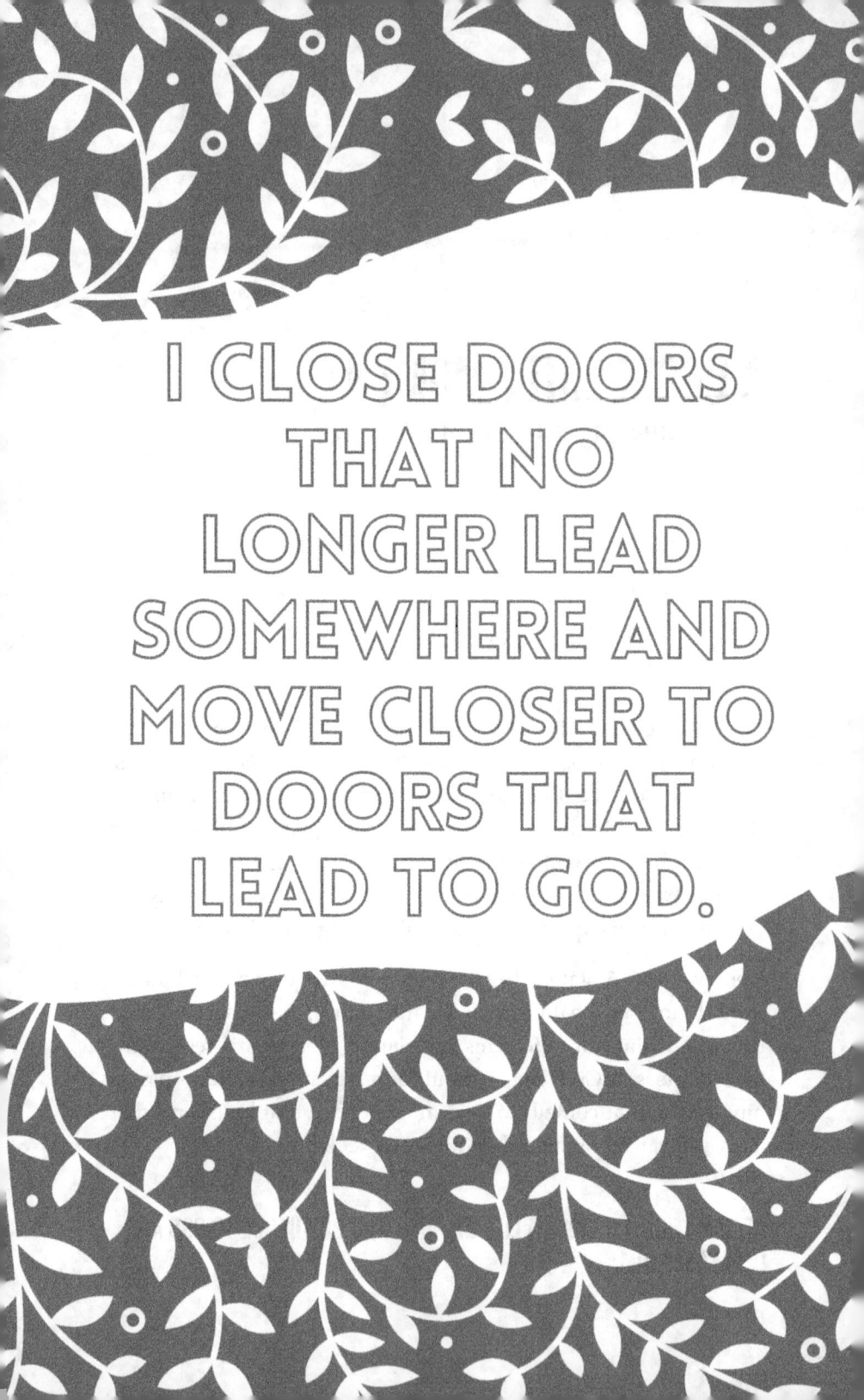

A PROSPERITY MOMENT
WITH SHANDRA PARKS

> Close some doors. Not because of pride, incapacity, or arrogance but simply because they no longer lead somewhere. - Paul Coelho

IN TODAY'S society we can often get caught up in doing a lot of things. We often have a tendency to too easily say yes to this or that. We even say yes when we should be saying no. As we are moving on our journey, there will be doors. Some are doors of opportunities. Others are doors of distractions. Some doors are meant to be opened while some are meant to be closed. We can close the doors that lead us away from God and close the doors that keep us from our purpose in life. Take a few minutes and reflect on the doors in your life. Can you see which doors need closing? Can you see the doors God is opening on your behalf as your draw closer to Him? Go to Him.

AFFIRMATION: I CLOSE DOORS THAT NO LONGER LEAD SOMEWHERE AND MOVE CLOSER TO DOORS THAT LEAD TO GOD.

I ALLOW GOD TO LEAD ME, SO I HAVE NO FEAR OF THE FUTURE.

A PROSPERITY MOMENT
WITH MINISTER TATONISHA VONSHA

> She is clothed with strength and dignity and laughs without fear of the future. - Proverbs 31:25

SPIRITUAL SUCCESS STARTS with your mind. If you have the mental strength to proclaim what is yours, you shall have what you say. This is how to build mental strength — nourish your inner man by reading the Word as if it's your last morsel of food. Then digest it so it can fill you up and give you fuel for your assignments. You guard your ears, eyes, & mouth knowing that you must protect the tools God has given you to hear, see, and speak to and for Him. Spend quiet time with God so you can know when, where, and how to move. And surround yourself with Him and surrender to the peace that comes with His presence. Then you can face every assignment "with strength and dignity" and "without fear of the future."

AFFIRMATION: I ALLOW GOD TO LEAD ME, SO I HAVE NO FEAR OF THE FUTURE.

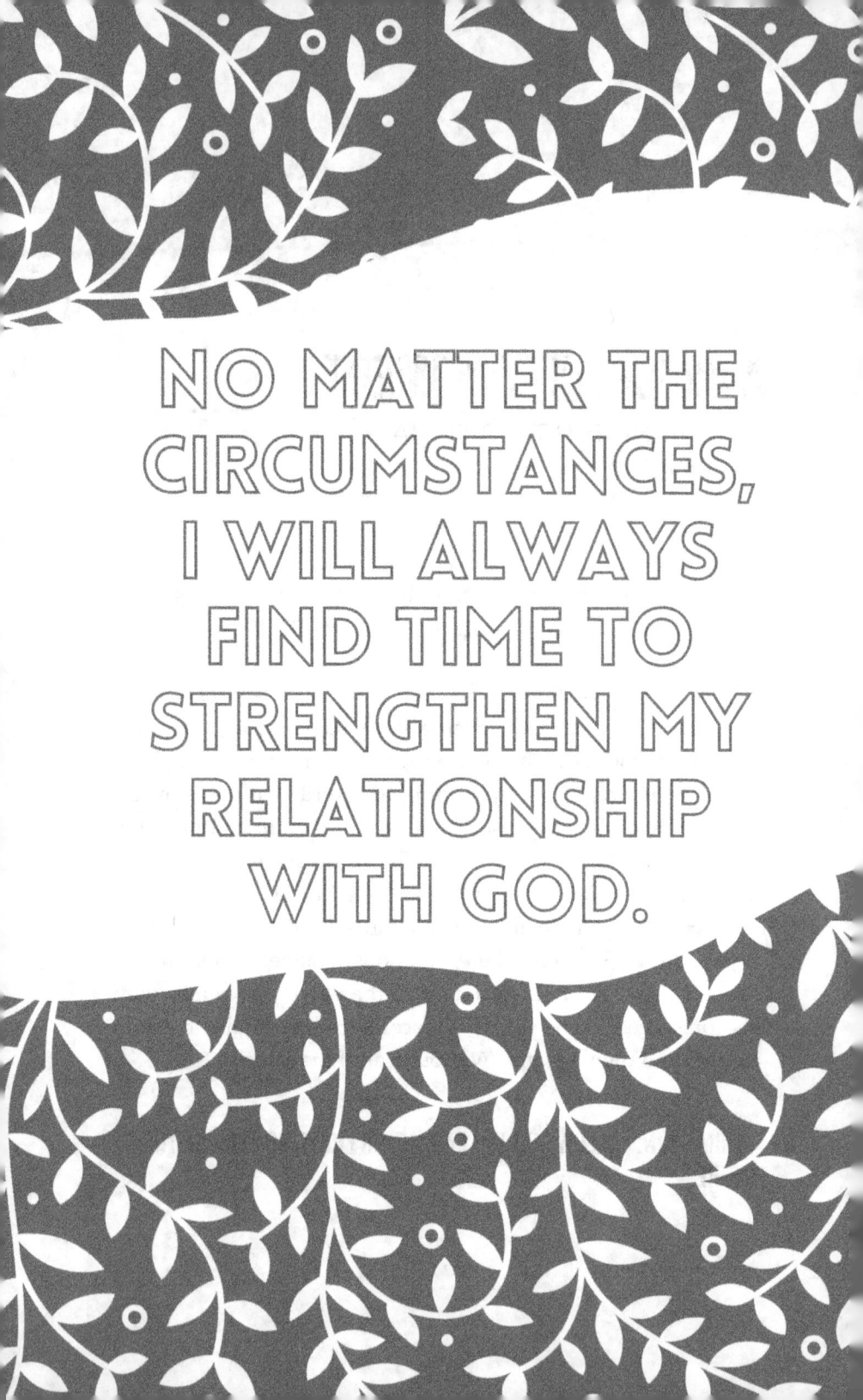

A PROSPERITY MOMENT
WITH DR. TSCHANNA TAYLOR

> But Martha was very busy *and* distracted with all of her serving responsibilities; and she approached Him and said, "Lord, is it of no concern to You that my sister has left me to do the serving alone? Tell her to help me *and* do her part. - Luke 10:40 AMP

DO you ever feel like Martha — distracted by many tasks? Busyness is different than faithfulness. Good things become bad things when they keep you from what's most important.

To achieve spiritual success in your life, only one thing is necessary and that's to spend time with God. Spending time with Jesus is an invitation to peace, joy, and success that can only be found in His presence. Without God, we can do nothing (John 15:5) and He has already equipped us with the tools for spiritual time management. It's up to us to make time for God so we can mount up with wings like an eagle and soar through our busy days with strength, strategy, and endurance.

AFFIRMATION: NO MATTER THE CIRCUMSTANCES, I WILL ALWAYS FIND TIME TO STRENGTHEN MY RELATIONSHIP WITH GOD.

GOD LOVES ME
SO DEEPLY THAT
HE TURNS MY
MISTAKES INTO
SOMETHING
GOOD.

A PROSPERITY MOMENT
WITH TYRIA D. JONES

> And we know that all things work together for good to them that love God, to them who are the called according to his purpose. – Romans 8:28

WHEN GOD CREATED US, He gave us free will. In doing so, He knew, in His infinite wisdom, that there would be instances in our walk when we would make decisions that wouldn't please Him. Yet, He still loves us. Lamentations 3:22-23 explains it so beautifully, "The steadfast love of the Lord never ceases; his mercies never come to an end; they are new every morning; great is your faithfulness." This means that nothing you can do will cause God not to love you. When you mess up, He is always waiting with open arms and forgiveness. Not only does His love never cease, but he will use those mistakes and turn them into something good for your life. He doesn't waste anything that you experience. It's all part of who He created you to be and a part of your beautiful story.

AFFIRMATION: GOD LOVES ME SO DEEPLY THAT HE TURNS MY MISTAKES INTO SOMETHING GOOD.

PHYSICAL PROSPERITY

I PRAY THAT YOU BE IN GOOD HEALTH.

HEALTH:

1 to have sound health, i.e. be well (in body);

2 figuratively, to be uncorrupt (true in doctrine)

3 to be in health, (be safe and) sound, (be) whole(-some).

— Lexicon :: Strong's G5198 - hygiainō

I WILL REST FROM MY LABOR AND GOD WILL TAKE CARE OF ME.

A PROSPERITY MOMENT
WITH ALLISON DENISE ARNETT

> Sometimes the best solution is to rest, relax, and recharge. It's hard to be your best on empty. ~ Sam Glenn

BURNOUT LOOKS a lot like mental and physical exhaustion. It feels like "I've gone as far as I can go." It feels like the world is moving faster by the day, everyone wants everything now, and I feel compelled to comply… or else. What can you pour from an empty cup? Nothing. This is the opposite of the abundant life God designed for us. If your body is exhausted, it cannot prosper. Psalms 127:2 says, "It is useless for you to work so hard from early morning until late at night, anxiously working for food to eat; for God gives rest to his loved ones." Even He, as the Creator of the Universe, took time to rest. So when you go to bed, both, lay down *and* sleep and let God work things out. The world will wait and tomorrow the sun will rise and we will try again - rested and refreshed.

AFFIRMATION: I WILL REST FROM MY LABOR AND GOD WILL TAKE CARE OF ME.

EVEN AS I COME AND GO I WILL PAUSE FOR THE CAUSE OF TAKING CARE OF MYSELF.

A PROSPERITY MOMENT
WITH CIARA SHANAE

> And He said to them, "Come aside by yourselves to a deserted place and rest a while." For there were many coming and going, and they did not even have time to eat. ~Mark 6:31 NKJV

HAVE you ever gotten so caught up in doing "all the things" that you forgot to eat? I have. And I wondered how do I manage to schedule everyone else in but neglect to make time for myself. Eating is not a luxury. It's a necessity!

I love how Jesus gently guided His disciples to partake in a practice that He followed himself (Matthew 14:23). When we find ourselves "coming and going" we must learn to slow down and implement self-care. As you are out here saving and serving your world, don't forget to have moments of stillness; times when you can turn off and really relax (see Psalms 23:2.) Let's be kind to ourselves, treat ourselves, and enjoy ourselves! If Jesus can find time for self-care, so can we!

AFFIRMATION: EVEN AS I COME AND GO I WILL PAUSE FOR THE CAUSE OF TAKING CARE OF MYSELF.

I CHOOSE TO LOVE ME.

A PROSPERITY MOMENT
WITH CLARICE MAY CREGGER

 It is okay to choose and love you. - Clarice May Cregger

BE gentle with yourself and remember it is okay to choose you. It is okay to love you. It is okay to give yourself permission to rest. Rest is important because God did not create us to be on the go all day long. For you to be able to express and show your love to others, you must learn to love you first. God said in Mark 12:31 "You shall love your neighbor as yourself. There is no other command greater than these." Allow yourself to get to know you, be okay with the growth you have developed, and accept whatever season you're in.

AFFIRMATION: I CHOOSE TO LOVE ME.

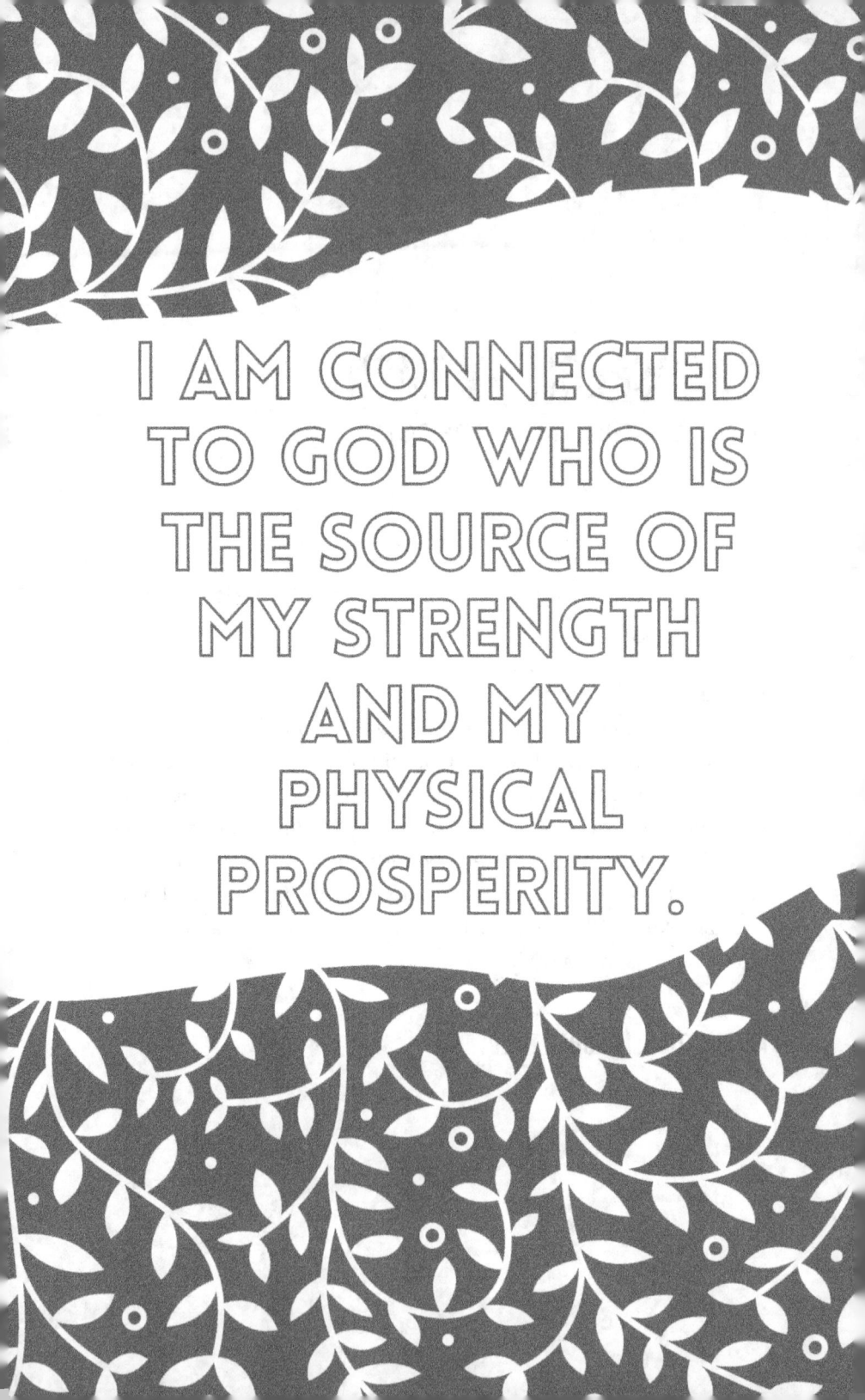

A PROSPERITY MOMENT
WITH CLARISSA PRITCHETT

> As for every man to whom God has given riches and many good things, He has also given him the power to eat from them, receive his reward and be happy in his work. This is the gift of God. – Ecclesiastes 5:19 (NLV)

DO NOT SACRIFICE physical health for wealth. God wants you to experience prosperity physically too. He wants you to show His glory financially, physically, and spiritually. Make physical exercise and eating healthy apart of your daily life. Believe in yourself and surround yourself people who support your well-being. Consume healthy and nutritious foods for your physical health and God's Word for your mental health daily. He has given you so many physical gifts! Stretch your arms to God daily and thank Him for your healthy and strong body. Take deep breaths of gratitude and exhale all disbelief. Choose happiness and feel greater physical prosperity entering your life.

AFFIRMATION: I AM CONNECTED TO GOD WHO IS THE SOURCE OF MY STRENGTH AND MY PHYSICAL PROSPERITY.

GOD'S HEALING LIGHT AND LIFE ARE COURSING THROUGH ME NOW.

A PROSPERITY MOMENT
WITH REV. CURTIS THATCHER

> Then shall thy light break forth as the morning, and thine health shall spring forth speedily. — Isaiah 58:8 KJV.

HEALTH IS MORE natural than illness and being at ease is more natural than being in pain. When you need healing, calm down, let go of any fears, and let God's healing light and life flow through you. Believe that God has given you the power to heal whatever needs to be fixed. Be filled with the healing light that goes through every cell and fiber of your body. God is bigger than any sign of sickness and when you say that God's power is working in and through you right now, healing light comes out. First in your mind, then in your body and you will get better quickly. Every moment, be thankful for the healing light and life of God that is inside of you. Then your light will shine like the sun rising and your healing will come quickly.

AFFIRMATION: GOD'S HEALING LIGHT AND LIFE ARE COURSING THROUGH ME NOW.

I ESTABLISH AND MAINTAIN HEALTHY HABITS.

A PROSPERITY MOMENT
WITH DEBORAH RIVERS DECOTEAU

HOW DIFFICULT IS it for you to find time to include physical activities in your daily life? Yes. I said daily. Unhealthy eating, lack of exercise, and lack of good sleep, result in an unhealthy body. Know that an overall healthy life is a part of God's will for you.

A good daily routine could look like at least 10-45 minutes of exercise or stretching. Be intentional as to what and when you eat and supplement with vitamins to compensate for the nutrients you're not getting from your food. You might also try fasting to allow your body time to heal itself. Reject any obstacles that try to come against your wellness efforts. A good routine will ensure you have the energy needed to live life on purpose for GOD. Let's put in the work for our bodies to be as healthy as our souls are becoming.

AFFIRMATION: I ESTABLISH AND MAINTAIN HEALTHY HABITS.

I WILL TAKE GOOD CARE OF THIS TEMPLE GOD HAS TRUSTED ME WITH.

A PROSPERITY MOMENT
WITH GEMMA BROWNE

> Don't you realize that your body is the temple of the Holy Spirit, who lives in you and was given to you by God? You do not belong to yourself. - 1 Corinthians 6:19

OUR BODIES ARE the temples of God therefore we should make every effort to care for them. Some fundamental things we can do to be great caretakers of this temple He has entrusted us with. Start bay keeping your mind free from stress and worry by leaning on God and trusting in His Word. Choose your foods wisely and eat well to give your body the fuel it needs. And something many people lack the most — rest. Take time to rest by getting enough sleep. And last but certainly not least, enjoy the life that God has given to you. Spend time with people you love doing things you love.

AFFIRMATION: I WILL TAKE GOOD CARE OF THIS TEMPLE GOD HAS TRUSTED ME WITH.

I THANK GOD FOR THE GIFT OF FORGIVENESS.

A PROSPERITY MOMENT
WITH JANENE DHALAI

> He will wipe away every tear from their eyes... there will be no more grief, crying, or suffering, because the first things have gone away — Revelation 21:4 KJV

HOLISTIC HEALING BEGINS with holistic forgiveness. When you leave an unpleasant circumstance to God, you give and receive the gift of forgiveness. This is not to say that you condone what occurred; rather, you have chosen to let it go. Your history only has the influence over you that you let it. You can either let your history hold you back or you can go forward. You can carry the weight of mental agony indefinitely or you can lay it down and give it to God. Make the decision to be free of bitterness, wrath, and hurt. As you let go of the agony of the past, claim the peaceful existence you deserve. Let your burdens lighten, your sorrows subside, and your heart expand. Let forgiveness allow you to laugh, love, and live a joyful life.

AFFIRMATION: I THANK GOD FOR THE GIFT OF FORGIVENESS.

GOD GIVES ME THE STEPS TOWARDS GOOD HEALTH.

A PROSPERITY MOMENT
WITH LINDA KENNARD

> Beloved I wish above all things that thou mayest prosper and be in health, even as thy soul prospereth. - 3 John 1:2

GOD ENCOURAGES us to be healthy. He is concerned about our whole being. Though it can be quite challenging sometimes, good health is obtainable because we can do all things through Christ who gives us the strength. Many times it takes offering the body up as a living sacrifice to God. Rom 12:1. Yes, sometimes you may fall off the band wagon but do not lose hope or give up. You can do this! He is our Helper, Comforter, and Trainer. We can ask the Holy Spirit to give us a desire for the right foods for our body and to make the right movements for our body. Take baby steps and don't be too hard on yourself. It takes 30 days to form a habit so master consistency and repetition. Remember, everything that concerns you, He will perfect it. Just ask Him.

AFFIRMATION: GOD GIVES ME THE STEPS TOWARDS GOOD HEALTH.

I LIVE FREELY AND LIGHTLY IN GOD.

A PROSPERITY MOMENT
WITH MONIQUE MOORER

> Come to Me, all of you who are weary and burdened, and I will give you rest. - Matthew 11:28

YOU DON'T USUALLY PLAN to stress. Sometimes the day just does not go as you thought it would. Did you know that having consistent stressful situations can actually affect your natural body? It can lead to increased stress hormone levels and can leave you feeling disheveled, uneasy, and heavy. We may end up asking ourselves how we got there.

The good news is that we serve a God that loves to love on His children. In Mathew 11:28-30 MSG, God's word asks "Are you tired? Worn out?" It then goes on to tell you what to do. It says "Come to me... and I'll show you how to take a real rest." It reminds us that during stressful moments, we can give our stressors over to God. He can handle anything and everything for us and with us. So rest in God's Word and "you'll learn to live freely and lightly".

AFFIRMATION: I LIVE FREELY AND LIGHTLY IN GOD.

I WILL LISTEN TO MY BODY AND PRIORITIZE MY HEALTH.

A PROSPERITY MOMENT
WITH NADIA MORALES

> I believe that the greatest gift that you can give your family and the world is a healthy you. - Joyce Meyer

AS LEADERS, we often push ourselves to make things work at the expense of our health. We take our bodies for granted, we chug coffee multiple times a day, sleep late, and maybe even stress eat on junk food and sweets when things go wrong.

We forget that we can only do things that our bodies let us do. We forget that our physical bodies are tools to create, serve, and worship. Without this tool, how can we be a living witness to the one true God?

Today, I encourage you to find balance in taking care of your body and working on your dreams. God values hard work, but He also made the Sabbath for a reason. If He believes that rest is essential, wouldn't He love it if you take care of yourself more?

AFFIRMATION: I WILL LISTEN TO MY BODY AND PRIORITIZE MY HEALTH.

I BELIEVE IN MYSELF AND MY GOALS AND SO DOES GOD MY FATHER !

A PROSPERITY MOMENT
WITH MINISTER PESHON ALLEN

> When the road is difficult with impossibilities, keep pushing forward to achieve your goals no matter what. Because the reward will always outweigh the obstacles. ~ Joseph Marshall Goodman, III

GOING after your your goals can sometimes feel like climbing a huge mountain. It takes all of your drive and mental capacity. You start out on fire and then start second guessing yourself wondering if you should just give up and let it go. But then you remember your goal and the spark to continue returns. It is then that you must fan the flames of your faith, push past doubt, and know that you can accomplish your goals! Psalm 121:1 says, "I will lift up mine eyes unto the hills, from whence cometh my help." Look to God for your strength and strategy and He will cause you to have good success with all those creative and witty ideas He gave you.

AFFIRMATION: I BELIEVE IN MYSELF AND MY GOALS AND SO DOES GOD MY FATHER!

I WILL REMAIN
IN THE PEACE OF
GOD.

A PROSPERITY MOMENT
WITH SHANDRA PARKS

> Peace I leave with you, my peace I give unto you: not as the world giveth, give I unto you. Let not your heart be troubled, neither let it be afraid. John 14:27

EVERYTHING HAS CHANGED. How we interact with each other. How we shop. How we communicate and what we tolerate. For many of us how we work has changed and even how we fellowship in our faith communities has changed. Celebrations are different and even how we grieve has changed. But even in the midst of all this change, peace is possible. The world will never be the same again and neither will we. Things have changed, but God is still the same. This has been a period of correction and of adjusting to a new way of being. Don't despise this space we are in though. And definitely do not run from it. Instead, flow with it because our steps are ordered by God. Know that all things are working out for our good. Remember to breathe, laugh, rest, pray, pause, and stay connected.

AFFIRMATION: I WILL REMAIN IN THE PEACE OF GOD.

AS GOD TAKES CARE OF MY SOUL, I AM DISCIPLINED TO TAKE CARE OF MY BODY DAILY.

A PROSPERITY MOMENT
WITH DR. TSCHANNA TAYLOR

> Don't you know that your body is a sanctuary of the Holy Spirit who is in you, whom you have from God? You are not your own - 1 Corinthian 6:19

YOU MAY BE busy raising a family and running a ministry or business. This has you getting up early to pray, staying up late to work, overwhelmed, frustrated, burning the candle at both ends, and disregarding the most valuable person ever — *YOU*!

Well, you're not alone. Physical success can be a constant struggle for many. Consistency gets put on the back burner because we are so busy. However, mastery of our health is important. We are meant to nourish our whole being — body, mind, and soul. The management of our whole being has a domino effect in every other area of our lives. Pray about everything concerning your physical success and follow the techniques Holy Spirit gives you so you can prosper in all things *and* be in good health.

AFFIRMATION: AS GOD TAKES CARE OF MY SOUL, I AM DISCIPLINED TO TAKE CARE OF MY BODY DAILY.

I AM
IMPORTANT
AND I TAKE TIME
FOR ME SO I
CAN BE MY BEST.

A PROSPERITY MOMENT
WITH TYRIA D. JONES

> For ye are bought with a price: therefore glorify God in your body; and in your spirit, which are of God's. – 1 Corinthians 6:20

IN THE BUSYNESS OF LIFE, we tend to focus on what everyone around us needs and we forget to take care of ourselves. We go for days and even months without stopping to do a self-check. Over the last few years, we've heard a lot about self-care and why it's important. Have you given any thought to how this applies to you? When was the last time you took a "me" day? Have you ever taken one? You're juggling so many things and always put yourself on the back burner. If you continue like this, instead of stopping on your own, your body can and may do it for you. It's time to put yourself first! It is only then that you will be at your best for everyone else in your life. It isn't selfish, but it is definitely necessary. Start prioritizing yourself today and set time aside each week for self-care.

AFFIRMATION: I AM IMPORTANT AND I TAKE TIME FOR ME SO I CAN BE MY BEST.

ENCOURAGE ONE ANOTHER

THEREFORE ENCOURAGE AND COMFORT ONE ANOTHER AND BUILD UP ONE ANOTHER, JUST AS YOU ARE DOING. - 1 THESSALONIANS 5:11

ENCOURAGE

1 to console, to encourage and strengthen by consolation, to comfort

2 to receive consolation, be comforted

3 to encourage, strengthen

4 exhorting and comforting and encouraging

5 to instruct, teach

— Lexicon :: Strong's G3870 - parakaleō

ALLISON DENISE ARNETT
VISIONARY AUTHOR AND PUBLISHER

CHRISTIAN MINISTER & TEACHER • AUTHOR BRAND STRATEGIST • INTERNATIONAL SPEAKER • BEST-SELLING AUTHOR • SPIRITUAL EMPOWERMENT COACH

Hi! I'm Allison Denise and I am in love with empowering Women in Ministry to align with their Kingdom assignments and leave their legacy in the world via books and influential author brands!

I started out in full-time business seven years ago after being wrongfully terminated by my employer one week after giving birth to my third child... we can talk more about that later. But that was the push I needed from God to step into my destiny. I am a degreed accountant who went back to her first love... CREATIVITY!

I published my first book in 2015 and now I am a 13x Best Selling Author. I gave my life to Christ at the age of 18 and was licensed and ordained as a minister in 2019. As the Creative Director & Designer of Author Brands, I have since empowered almost 200 women to self-publish and become bestsellers of transformational books as well. Every book I release or event I host encourages women leaders to stand in their God-designed feminine authority in their minds, ministries, and in the marketplace.

We are not just publishing books.

We are transforming lives.

Empowering women leaders is my ministry.

Writing, designing, & releasing books is my assignment.

You are my assignment.

If you are a ministry-minded, woman leader who's ready to publish your book, expand your ministry, and advance God's Kingdom — connect with me.

Website: www.BrandItBeautifully.com

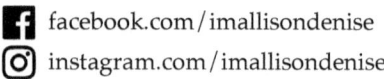

facebook.com/imallisondenise
instagram.com/imallisondenise

CEDRIC STANTON

Cedric Stanton was born on May 16, 1981, in Mound Bayou, MS. Throughout high school and college, Stanton struggled which caused him to become fearful of completing his education. While in high school, his first job was at RL Arron's LTD. He was passionate about working as an intern at the Children's Defense Fund Freedom School. Refusing to be beaten, he pushed himself to overcome his fears. Determined to live by his motto to not settle for less, he pursued his dreams and finished college. He successfully obtained his bachelor's degree from Rust College in Holly Spring, MS.

In 2013, he started his business called Cedman's Divine Creations where he does graphic design and paints portraits. He has also been called into ministry and continues to lead people to the kingdom of God.

CIARA SHANAE

Ciara Shanae is a Sought-after Speaker, Best-selling Author, and Brand Visibility Strategist at Pro-Visement, LLC, her Brand Communications Firm. Through her Voice to Clients Method™, she absolutely loves to teach powerhouse speakers how to amplify their voice so they can boost their visibility, grow their tribe, and enroll clients on repeat. With her background being in Psychology, it is no surprise to her when she hears how therapeutic and empowering her coaching experiences are. When she is not speaking or working with speaker brands, you can find her spending time with her boss baby, Kaiden, attending events for fun, or watching some kind of romantic chick flick.

Connect on Instagram @iamciarashanae

Learn more at www.iamciarashanae.com

CLARICE MAY CREGGER

Clarice May Cregger (aka Coach Claire) is an international speaker, motivator, 2x #1 Amazon Bestselling Author, and the founder of the International Women's Empowerment Group "Broken But Beautifully Made LLC". She was born and raised in the Philippines and currently resides in Albuquerque, NM. Clarice has co-authored two books — "Heart of God for Her 45 Day Devotional" and "Give Me a Minute" and has written and published her very own book titled "Broken But Beautifully Made."

Clarice is a creative entrepreneur and as a Certified Life Coach, her focus is on breaking harmful patterns and overcoming guilt and shame. She is also CEO and Founder of ClaireMayPhotography & Designs LLC and the Co-Founder of G.UR.L. Geturlife Coaching, Consultation, and Training LLC.

CLARISSA PRITCHETT, M.P.H.

Clarissa Pritchett, M.P.H., is an Integrative Nutrition Health Coach, Empowerment Speaker, Author, Entrepreneur, and Army Medical Service Corps Officer. Clarissa is a wife and mom to three beautiful boys. Clarissa is passionate about health and wellness and has served numerous clients over the past 20 years. She has a Bachelor's degree in Health Education, a Masters Degree in Public Health Nutrition and numerous certifications in the fitness and nutrition field. She is an online health coach and self care coach who also mentors women to start online businesses while promoting Sisterhood, Self-Care, and Service to those in need. She loves to encircle and uplift women to live healthy lives. She has written numerous recipe and health guide eBooks. She is a sought after speaker and resilience instructor for the military, wellness companies, and local churches to where she shares her story of overcoming health and life challenges. She loves to motivate women with their health and life goals to prosper. Clarissa is a short, sweet, and spicy mixed salad sistah that keeps it real, raw and organic about how she overcame many health challenges and body issues. Overall, her favorite things in life are Jesus, family, friends, cooking and eating food, especially tacos, donuts and chocolate!

Connect on Instagram and Facebook @ClarissaHealthCoach

Join the Private Facebook Group: TheRealSelfLoveSisterhood

Get Free Fitness Tips and Healthy Recipes: www.ClarissaHealthCoach.com

REV. CURTIS ANDRE THATCHER

Rev. Curtis Andre Thatcher flows as spiritual director of Grace Amazing Foundation, Inc to minister to those afflicted by grief and trauma in 2021. Rev. Curtis teaches that there is much fruition when adopting leadership styles such as servant and transformational leadership. Nonetheless, the Trinity provides the doctrinal information for leading God's people; hence, the Scriptures are required to lead the way God expects ministers to do. Rev. Curtis is also a certified life coach. He engages in coaching and mentoring for Prison Ministry, provides para-pastoral support to Christian ministries, and promotes the mission for God's Kingdom. Rev. Curtis is married enjoys his children, family and friends.

DEBORAH RIVERS DECOTEAU

Deborah Rivers Decoteau is a 3x Best Selling Author, Wellness Director, and Caribbean Carnival Costume Designer and Band Leader. A native of Trinidad and Tobago, she has dedicated her life to bringing awareness to her culture via singing, dancing, and writing. It is her life's work to empower women to wellness, and to live a life by God's design. Deborah is a mother of five and is affectionately known by her grandchildren as Little G. When she is not adding building blocks to her legacy, you will find her in Houston, Texas crafting to keep her creative ideas flowing.

GEMMA BROWNE

Gemma Browne is an Early Childhood Educator, a calling she refers to as her mission field, especially as she works with teenage moms at the high school campus. She loves reading and books and has been married for 48 years to her husband Ronnie. She is the mother of three children and five grandchildren.

JANENE DHALAI

Janene Dhalai graduated from the University of the West Indies in Trinidad and Tobago with a certificate in Early Childhood Social and Emotional Developmental Programs. Furthermore, she earned a Bachelor of Science in Religion with a concentration in Christian Counseling and a minor in Psychology. Presently, Janene holds a master's degree in Human Services Counseling—Crisis and Trauma and is pursuing her Ph.D. in Traumatology. Finally, good communication is critical in my profession, personal relationships, and ministry. In addition, she assists grieving and traumatized persons as part of her contribution to her non-profit organization and missionary work.

LINDA KENNARD

Linda Kennard, an only child until adulthood, found out that she had two siblings — one of which she got to meet named Jerry. Her parents have been major blessings in her life and she honors and thanks God for them everyday. She is the mother of one beautiful daughter, Tangina, the grandmother of three, and great grandmother to children whom she loves dearly.

Linda has an associate's in Christian Counseling and a Bachelor's in Business Administration and has written several productions such as "New Breed 1&2" along with Amateur Night 1,2,3 and performed at the UWC Temple.

After receiving the Holy Spirit she became a true worshipper and since that time, so much has happened and is happening. So there's no ending to Linda's autobiography because she's still in progression...Phil 1:6

MONIQUE MEREDITH MOORER

Monique Meredith Moorer is a #1 Best Selling Author of a devotional anthology called "Heart of God for Her". Monique is a wife of a retired Army Master Sergeant and mother of three. She is a Licensed Practical Nurse for over twenty-four years. As a minister of God, she has served her local church in many capacities. An encourager at heart, her lively and vibrant personality can uplift almost any room. Monique wants to remind you that often we do not see it, but just like her, God has a specific plan and purpose with you in mind. Just take each day moment by moment.

NADIA MORALES

Nadia Morales spent most of her younger years pursuing her parents' dream of her becoming a doctor. She was doing her best to get the MD on her name until it felt like she wasn't being true to herself. She finished her degree in Biochemistry and became a licensed chemist so all her years science education wouldn't go down the drain. She later resigned from doing product development in the cosmetics industry to go for something more meaningful in her life.

She has since confirmed that God wanted her to do exactly what she's doing in this season: empowering online course creators by designing brands that communicate their expertise and crafting websites that serve their purpose.

Follow her on Instagram @hanancreatives or reach out to her for partnerships at nadia@hanancreatives.com.

PESHON ALLEN

Peshon Allen is a seasoned, passionate broadcaster who keeps her heart and fingers on the pulse of what's going on in the world around her. She is also a well sought-after worship leader, Army Veteran, alumnus of the American Forces Network in Germany, and a Believer in Jesus Christ.

Peshon is the CEO, Founder and Visionary behind the Radio Broadcast Show and Podcast called, "Women In Ministry On The Move!" that focuses on Women from all walks of life and the services they provide in ministry, at home, and in their communities. The show can be heard on all platforms and mobile devices. Peshon is married to the love of her life, Mr. Tyron Allen and together they adore two beautiful children.

Connect on Instagram and Facebook @peshonallen or on the web at www.peshonallen.com

SHANDRA PARKS, PHD, LMSW, CFSW, AFC CANDIDA

Dr. Parks is a Licensed Master Social Worker and has been working with children, youth, and families for the past 22 years in the areas of child welfare, community social work and ministry wellness. Dr. Parks has a desire to see individuals, families, and communities living healthy, whole and prosperous lives. Dr. Parks is the owner of Sparks Consulting Group which is a consulting firm providing coaching, training and financial education services. Dr. Parks holds a Bachelor's Degree in Social Work, Master's Degree in Social Work, Doctor of Philosophy in Clinical Christian Counseling. Dr. Parks also holds the following certifications in Financial Social Work, Clergy Problem Gambling Spiritual Outreach certification and currently an Accredited Financial Counselor Candidate. Dr. Parks is a member of Delta Sigma Theta Sorority, Incorporated. Dr. Parks serves the community in the following capacities: Vice-President with the Maryland Council on Problem Grambling and Financial Educator with the Annapolis/Anne Arundel Financial Education Coalition.

Contact on LinkedIn @ShandraParks

MINISTER TATONISHA VONSHA

Minister Tatonisha Vonsha Founder of G.E.M.S Girls Elevating and Mastering Success mentorship program for young girls. Having a heart for Empowering Woman. She is also the founder of Parent Foundation where she teaches single parents that their situation is not their final destination. Tatonisha Von'sha is the author of Mask Off "No More Hiding" which helped create her new Ministry "FreeFrom" which is an organization with a safe space for removing your mask to heal. For the last 5 years Tatonisha has accepted that Ministry life is where the peace lies so she is continuing to kingdom build, loving God like never before. She is a mother and a wife who resides in the Chicagoland area.

Connect: TatonishaVonsha.com

DR. TSCHANNA TAYLOR

Whereas others find their greatest fulfillment and motivation in moving forward, she found hers in looking *back*. Affectionately known as *"The Chief Fiyah Igniter"*, Dr. Tschanna Taylor realized to effectively build in her life, she had to heal hurts that stemmed from childhood. Dr. Tschanna is committed to helping others dig through roots in their life and confidently share their message to grow and bear fruits monetizing from their pain.

Dr. Tschanna is a publisher, TEDx speaker, marketplace chaplain, and an 18x International Best-Selling Author. Tschanna holds several degrees and certifications from Keller Graduate School of Management and other institutions, focusing on entrepreneurship. Set apart by her transparent delivery and transformative storytelling abilities, anyone can clearly see that she is resilient about helping others operate authentically and unapologetically in their purpose.

Connect @tschannataylor on Facebook and TikTok.

Visit her website at www.tschannataylor.com.

TYRIA D. JONES

Tyria D. Jones is married to the love of her life, Kenneith. Together they have 13 beautiful children. Tyria is a 3x Amazon Bestselling Author, Purpose Coach and Speaker.

In 2016, Tyria wrote her memoir, *A Crown of Beauty for Ashes*, she shared her journey from abuse and homelessness to a living a life of victory in God. Tyria is passionate about empowering women to be the best version of themselves so they too can live a victorious life. In her newest memoir, *Pain to Purpose: Escaping the F.I.R.E. to Get to Freedom* which launched January 2020, she shares how God healed her of past trauma and used her pain to launch her into the purpose He had for her life.

Tyria's other works include: *Broken Chains* and *Soul-to-Soul* anthologies as well as a companion 31-day devotional for *A Crown of Beauty for Ashes* and an e-book: *Overcoming Fear*.

MORE ENCOURAGEMENT

HERE ARE OTHER TITLES BY ALLISON DENISE ARNETT

VISIONARY AUTHOR OF:

Give Me A Minute

We Blaze the Trail

The Heart of God for Her

Love, Life, & Recklessness

Body Talk: Finding the Beauty in You

I Signed My Own Permission Slip

God Made Me Beautiful (Children's Book)

Plan to Publish - Self Publishers 90 Day Companion

CONTRIBUTING AUTHOR IN:

Unleash Your Undeniable Impact

The Perfect 7 Devotional

Belief, Boldness, & Big Blessings

Poised & Profitable

Visit: www.BrandItBeautifully.com/shop

If you are a ministry-minded, woman leader who's ready to publish your book, expand your ministry, and advance God's Kingdom — connect with Allison at www.BrandItBeautifully.com

www.ingramcontent.com/pod-product-compliance
Lightning Source LLC
Chambersburg PA
CBHW071854070526
44583CB00016B/1688